I Have Something To Say

I Have Something To Say

Rachel Dowdell, Author
Kate Bergeron, Cover Illustrator

Columbus, Ohio

I Have Something To Say

Published by Gatekeeper Press

2167 Stringtown Rd, Suite 109

Columbus, OH 43123-2989

www.GatekeeperPress.com

ISBN (paperback): 9781642375091

Printed in the United States of America

the table of contents

the acknowledgments

Thank you, Mom and Dad, for being so wonderfully supportive even when I wouldn't let you read anything I had written.

Thank you, Rebekah and Malachi, for being discreet when I did let you read what I had written.

Thank you, Omi and Grandpa, for being two of my biggest fans.

Thank you, Gramma, for constantly encouraging me.

Thank you Oma, for always supporting me.

Thank you, Kate, for your endless marketing expertise and always pushing me forward,

And thank You, God, for giving me this book to write.

To my Grandfather, Robert.

Thank you for being an
instrument of Grace.

Empowerment (n): the act or action of empowering someone or something: the granting of the power, right, or authority to perform various acts or duties.

Or in simpler terms:

Grace.

I love words. And this year, my favorite word is empowerment. So my hope is that you are empowered while reading this book. I hope that you are empowered to connect with those you would have once passed by, empowered to understand a different perspective, empowered to feel understood, and empowered to feel loved. But most of all, I hope that you are empowered to live the dazzling life that you were meant to live. You are a jewel - and I hope that this book empowers you to shine as bright as you can.

- Rachel Dowdell

<u>the introduction</u>

"Please be quiet, I'm trying to think."

What a funny phrase, this is. Trying to think.

Clearly, we are already thinking. We had to think in order to say the phrase "I'm trying to think".

Of course we do not really mean that we are "trying" to think. We are not "struggling" to think.

In reality, what we mean to say is:

"Shut up already, shut *up* and let me process the indecisiveness bombarding my mind so that I can create a coherent answer to your question!"

Yet all of these words are condensed to the vague and weak phrase:

"I'm trying to think."

It's a shame that not many people say what
they mean.

What a better world we would live in.

And not only better, but a more exciting,
more passionate world-

Maybe with less confusion, too.

Where peoples' words no longer fall flat and
lifeless like wet bread on the ground-

Where words are not just meaningless
syllables being stated over and over and over-

Where words will

Bloom

In my ear.

A world where, when you speak, everybody
stops to listen.

Where the words that come out of our

mouths are fire.

They are electric -

They are bold pulses -

They are Life.

I long to live in a world where the people
speak

Life.

Until then I sit.

I sit at my desk and think and filter through
the words around me -

Choosing, picking, selecting the words that
speak Life, that breathe Life into me.

I'm trying to think.

Dear one, be bold.

Spit fire, not ice.

When you speak, let your words be so filled
with so much Hope and Peace that people
flock to you. They surround you and beg you
to:

Speak Life, my friend, speak Life.

They are waiting for you to:

Speak Life, my friend, speak Life.

The world is waiting for you to:

Speak Life, my friend, speak Life.

I am waiting for you to:

Speak Life, dear one, speak Life.

You are far too powerful

To speak so weak.

How Lovely to be a

(Black)

Woman

<u>Raw never meant no sugar (although it did mean less cake)</u>

One day when I was twelve I looked at my black curly hair
and decided that I did not want black *curly* hair I wanted
black *straight* hair.

So I went to my mother with my best "Pretty please?" voice
and my best "Pretty please?" eyes and begged her to take my
curls away.

So one day my mother and I went to the salon. We sat with a
hairdresser

(The hairdresser had straight brown hair and I thought that
it was very pretty)

And four hours later I looked in the mirror and the black
curly hair was gone. I had black *straight* hair. And my
mother said, "Merry Christmas."

For so long I struggled with my hair. For a mixed girl there
was no clear-cut way to do my hair. Nobody knew what to
do with it.

My Mother (white) would smooth it down with cream.

My Father (black) would grease it up with oil.

My Grandmother (black) would use a hot comb and hot oil.

My other Grandmother (white) wouldn't care.

I (white and black) would slather on gel.

So, for so long I was constantly changing my hair.

Grades one through six: curly.

Grades six through nine: straight.

Grade ten: curly (I joined the swim team. Keeping my hair straight was impossible).

The spring of junior year: curly (Except for junior prom. That was too important).

Senior year fall: curly. Senior year spring: straight

(A boy I liked admitted to me that he thought I looked more attractive with straight hair. I spent the summer out of the pool).

Freshman year of college: straight

(Many girls complained of the smell of burning hair. I learned to straighten my hair late at night, when the bathroom was empty).

Maybe it was when I saw my roommate's hair

(She was mixed. Half black. Like me).

Maybe it was when I saw *my* hair

(Wet, but still straight).

Maybe it was when I had to scramble for an idea for my

history paper

(Based on finding identity).

But one day I looked in the mirror and I no longer saw black curly hair and I no longer saw black straight hair. I saw a mix.

And I asked myself:

"Who are you?"

And my reflection answered:

"Whoever you want me to be."

"No, I mean…. black or white. Who are you?"

And I stared at myself, and years of being called half and half, zebra, and Oreo crashed in on me. Yet my reflection only blinked.

One day I asked my Mother (white), who I was.

"My daughter," she replied.

"No, I mean…black or white. Which am I?"

"Black."

"That's it?"

"My dear, that is *everything*."

One day I looked in the mirror and I no longer saw a girl struggling with hair. One day I looked in the mirror and saw a woman staring back at me.

"Who are you?"

My reflection only blinked.

I asked again:

"Who *are* you?"

But I didn't get an answer. And I didn't get an answer for a very long time.

But one day I looked in the mirror, and I said to my reflection:

"More than a comment. More than a hairstyle. And more than a color. That is who you are."

My reflection blinked. And my reflection asked:

"More than enough?"

One day I stared at my reflection. I saw a woman (black) with black curly hair. I smiled. And I told myself:

"You are more than enough."

<u>Ladies That Slay</u>

I will be a lady that slays.

The day

The month

The year

There will not be a day

That I do not slay.

I will be strong

Fierce

Brave.

I will

Slay.

My job

My relationships

Everything that comes my way

I will

Slay.

Do you say-

I cannot slay?

Bite

Your tongue.

In rain,

I slay.

In sun,

I slay.

At night,

I slay.

And in day,

I slay.

You cannot touch me.

Take a step back

For my punches swing wide

And

Let's be honest

You cannot contain

The way that I slay.

<u>Blight History Month</u>

I saw him on the runway -

The MC -

And I remember thinking:

"Poor guy. His hands are shaking holding that microphone. He's nervous."

And why shouldn't he be?

It was February 10.

Black History Month.

We were at a black fashion show.

He was a black man on a gray stage speaking to a dark audience.

Only the lights were white.

"Who would've thought that one day we could make it here?" he shouted. His face dripped with sweat. "Who would've thought that one day we could all make it *here*?"

The audience roared. And his sweat hit the runway-

Clear and bright.

And it was the same sweat felt by millions and millions of black people who had to stand in front of a crowd and convince the world that we were worth more.

It was the same sweat felt by all the black men and black women who spoke out to a crowd about black beauty and excellence.

It was the same sweat that poured down Martin Luther King Jr.'s face –

The same sweat that dripped down Frederick Douglass's brow.

And as the sweat hit the floor and as the audience continued to roar I looked around me –

And on the walls were ten portraits.

Ten pairs of white eyes staring back at me.

And as the audience continued to cheer I saw the eyes stare in amusement.

"Silly black folk," they said. "They think they fill this space. But don't they know we own the building they occupy? Don't they know we own the space they fill?"

The audience kept clapping. The eyes kept smiling.

"So let us celebrate a night of true Afro-culture!" The MC shouted -

And the white eyes only laughed.

<u>If I Marry a Black Man</u>

Suppose I marry a black man.

Suppose his name is Deshawn or Tyrone or Tyrell –

Suppose I marry a black man.

Suppose I call him ebony and suppose he calls me ivory
and we laugh –

Suppose his laugh is deep.

Suppose we have children –

They will be darker than me.

Suppose I have a daughter –

Suppose we name her Latisha.

Suppose I marry a black man and suppose I meet his
black family.

Suppose at every family gathering we eat fried chicken,
mac and cheese, and watermelon.

Suppose we all drink sweet tea.

Suppose my Mother-in-Law calls me "sugar" and says
"sookie sookie."

Suppose I marry a black man.

Suppose I stand next to him at the altar -

Suppose we exchange vows.

Suppose, ten years later, while I'm making mac and cheese and cutting watermelon and our son is playing basketball and our oldest daughter is braiding our youngest daughter's hair, I tell him I'm pregnant again.

Suppose he smiles and laughs and cries and hugs me –

And suppose I bury my face in his dark chest, and breathe deep –

Suppose I smell cedar wood.

I sit across from you, now.

We are on the T and it is crowded.

Your hoodie and headphones blend in with your skin.

I see my reflection in the passing window –

Pale chocolate.

Suppose I marry a black man –

Would I be black enough for him?

If I Marry a White Man

Suppose I marry a white man.

Suppose his name is Tom or John or Rick –

Suppose I marry a white man.

Suppose I call him ivory and he calls me ebony and we
laugh–

Suppose his laugh is light.

Suppose we have children –

They will be lighter than me.

Suppose I have a daughter –

Suppose we name her Tiffany.

Suppose I marry a white man and suppose I meet his white
family.

Suppose at every family gathering we eat salad, quinoa, and
cheese.

Suppose we all drink purified water.

Suppose my Mother-In-Law calls me "sweetheart" and says
"Tots adorbs."

Suppose I marry a white man.

Suppose I stand next to him at the altar –

Suppose we exchange vows.

Suppose, ten years later, while I'm making salad and cooking quinoa and our son is playing lacrosse and our oldest daughter is doing Pilates with our youngest daughter, I tell him I'm pregnant again.

Suppose he smiles and laughs and cries and hugs me –

And suppose I bury my face in his pale chest, and breathe deep –

Suppose I smell lemon grass.

I sit across from you, now.

We are on the T and it is crowded.

Your coral polo is stark against your pale skin.

I see my reflection in the passing window –

Dark caramel.

Suppose I marry a white man –

Would I be white enough for him?

<u>But Hughes Said-</u>

I sat in the class – silent and angry.

I was listening to a man tell me what a black writer
meant by his words.

And I sat there,

Silent and angry,

Wanting to say:

"Well no *duh* he was advocating for equality. Of *course*
he felt a double consciousness, of *course* he wanted to be
successful no *duh*, he was a black man among a sea of
white, do you know how scary that can be? Being a
shadow against a white backdrop? Black like oil on a
wedding dress, bathed in the bright lights of a police
station, feeling ever more prominent while against a wall
of white? Lost like a dog in a blurring snow?"

But I didn't. I just sat there and kept listening.

Because I couldn't read that deep into the author's
words.

My white teacher read them better.

No Longer Slaves (?)

I can see the weight on their shoulders. The pain and the
rejection.

I can see the years of shame in their eyes.

When they walk, their shoulders slump forward, as if

The generations and generations of field labor are still their
way of life.

I can see the weight of the stigma-

In the slow heavy walk, in the fast light feet, that they are
still trying to run away, they are still trying to find the
North Star, they are still searching for the railroad to point
them to freedom.

They are still waiting.

They are still watching the skies waiting for the drinking
gourd, waiting for the sky to dip, dip,

They are waiting.

They are still walking that dirt road.

They are still running and searching and hiding.

They are still seeking their freedom.

They are still longing to be free.

<u>Fierce Femininity (Flower Power isn't just for hippies anymore)</u>

Amaryllis.

Since when did being feminine equate to being weak?

Back in Sparta, the woman was considered to be as strong as the man.

Since when did wearing lipstick make me a whore?

I like my lips red.

In fact, when did wearing dresses and high heels and makeup and smelling good make me somehow

Weak? Ineffective? And

Only perceived as a giant flirt?

To all the ladies, who have gone out and worn:

Power suits, scrubs, fatigues, lab coats, space suits, overalls, coveralls, freezer suits, hard hats, and ties-

I say thank you.

To all the ladies, who have gone out and worn:

Aprons, old pajamas, macaroni necklaces, spit stains,

vomit and urine and dirt and blood and tears-

I say thank you.

And to all of the ladies, who have worn:

All of this,

And *more* -

I say thank you.

And to all of the ladies, who, at one time or another,
have been handed

The stigma. The shame of being a woman. The
perception that they are not good enough, that they are
weak, that they are not enough, that they are only
second best-

I apologize.

I apologize

That others could not and would not

See you for the fierce flower you are.

Amaryllis. You beautiful soul.

You have come so far.

You have accomplished so much.

And there is so much more to be done.

So roll up your sleeves:

And fix that hair (or not, my hair won't allow much fixing), put on that lipstick (I also like Chapstick), slip on those shoes (I'm partial to being barefoot but heels work too), pick up that sword (whether it be your briefcase, your stethoscope, your pen, your calculator, your spatula, or your paintbrush)

And show this world that

Regardless

Of what they think

You are:

A force to be reckoned with. The one and only you. Unique. Powerful. Wonderful. Stunningly creative. Full of ingenuity. Intelligent beyond *belief-*

Excuse my clichés

But you are far too good to have anybody-

(yes, anybody. That means you too)-

Sell yourself so short.

Amaryllis.

No one ever underestimated the power of a dragon.

Why should anyone ever underestimate the power of
you?

<u>Tough As Nails (gel nails, of course)</u>

On the swim team –

We would travel –

To small towns.

Small, rural towns.

Small, white towns.

And we were a bus of nations.

On those rides I chose to listen to my blackest music.

I hate rap –

But I would listen to rap.

I would listen to rap and gaze out the window looking
as tough as I could.

I walked off the bus with more pride.

As a wave of color washed through the pale sea

I remember thinking:

"Show these people what it means to be black."

If only I could go back

To tell myself that, even then,

I didn't know what it meant to be black.

We swam anyways.

#adulting

<u>BBN</u>

As a kid, I went for a lot of car rides with my Dad.

I loved those car rides.

I would love to go on car rides with my Dad and my sister –

The car always had a faint, sickly sweet smell...

Like melted crayon.

Maybe it was melted crayon.

In the car, my Dad and my sister and I would all play Better Brand News.

BBN, for short.

We would report on the truly important things in life.

"Mrs. Thompson just had another healthy baby!"

"Today a local man won ten *billion* dollars!"

"The sun is shining, the air is warm – today is shaping up to be a *great* day."

You know. Those stories.

And if we ever got stuck for a story, if we ever just needed one good thing to say, we would just tell each other:

"Have another cup of coffee."

Today I stare at the news.

"The government has shut down."

"Police find children trapped inside a house."

"Tensions in North Korea are rising."

I tune it out and close my eyes and picture the car.

I smell the scent of old crayons and wet shoes -

And I look out the kitchen window.

The sun is rising and it looks warm.

"Today is going to be a great day," I tell myself and I reach for another cup of coffee.

Red light, green light bridge.

You fell apart two years ago. And when you broke, I remember thinking:

"That was a good bridge."

And when they rebuilt you- they changed you-

Into something that you weren't.

Something we didn't want you to be.

I didn't recognize the wood they used.

And when we drove by, nobody said your name. Nobody called (with glee)

"Red light green light bridge!"

No.

We were all just silent –

And drove by in disgust.

I wish we could rebuild you.

<u>Lamprius- the Prius of lambs</u>

I can still smell the theater-

And still see all its chairs-

I can see my scarf on the floor over there-

I can see my shoes, stuck under the stage,

And I see the director-

Untouched by age.

He shouts and he screams but by the end of the night-

When he shuts off all the theater lights-

All we do is wait,

And sit,

And sigh,

Because once these doors close-

We know we can't go back again.

So quietly,

Silently,

And sullenly,

We close the heavy curtain and take our final bow.

<u>Uber</u>

The silence was heavier than I wanted it to be.

I kept my head,

Turned to the right-side window,

Afraid to move.

Because if I turned I may have caught your glance in the rear view mirror and I would have felt pressured to talk.

Maybe it was because there was a gulf between us.

Or maybe I only imagined the gulf between us.

Maybe you were just like me.

Maybe you had once been a college student catching rides to go home for the weekend maybe you had once studied James Joyce in the early hours and maybe you had once liked to look out the window and think.

I can feel the gulf between us.

But maybe it's not there.

Maybe I'm just putting it there what if I'm just like the construction workers teeming throughout the city maybe I just keep building walls upon walls upon walls until between every person I meet there is a gulf.

There are gulfs between us.

When the ride is over I thank you profusely -

As if you are an old friend who has helped me out or -

As if you are the friendly Samaritan who has lifted me up.

You just nod.

And as I leave the car,

I second guess every word unsaid every blink every pause
every silence that said nothing

Yet said everything.

Even you felt the gulfs between us.

I look at my Uber rating.

You gave me five stars.

Do they represent the space you felt between us?

I give you five stars back.

<u>Disconnected</u>

It was Thanksgiving.

We sat at the table in tense silence –

The kind of tense silence you always hate to see in movies because it is so awkward –

Yet you love to see in movies because it is so awkward.

We sat in that kind of tense silence.

The food was warm, and it smelled good –

And I distinctly remember cranberry bread –

Sitting on my plate.

It looked delicious.

"What do you *mean* you *don't* support our President?" My family asked. Their faces were shocked.

And confused.
And even though their mouths didn't move their eyes did and said:

"But this isn't how we raised you!"

In the kitchen the coffee pot beeped. Outside a bird chirped and inside my cousin dropped his fork.

He was only five.

"I'm sorry," I said. "I only meant to say-"

"No." The eyes at the table scolded me. "You don't get a say in this."

My cousin dropped his fork again. The eyes kept scolding and the food kept cooling.

I picked up my plate and moved to the children's table,

Where I belonged.

"You sit here?" My cousin asked.

"Yes." My family's heads nodded. "She sits there."

They went back to talking. I looked at my cranberry bread. I just wanted to eat.

It was Thanksgiving.

<u>Her</u>

Tell me I'm beautiful.

Tell me I'm the most beautiful woman you've ever known.

Tell me that I'm beautiful even when I don't feel beautiful.

Tell me you love me.

Tell me you admire me –

Tell me you desire me –

Tell me I'm not only a body.

Tell me you see more than a figure and if you only see a figure tell me see Artemis or Athena –

Tell me I'm not Venus.

Tell me I'm worth more.

Tell me that I'm more than enough, I'm always enough

And I will forever and always be enough for you.

Tell me that even when my beauty fades you will still be deeply in love with me.

Tell me you know me.

Tell me you know the color of my eyes

And the shape of my hair and the tone of my sighs –

Tell me you won't leave me.

Tell me you won't leave me for *her*, tell me you won't look at *her*, you won't be with *her*, tell me you won't abandon *our* life for *her* life.

Tell me you won't leave me.

Tell me I don't need a job –

But I can have a job and I'm great at my job –

But I don't need a job.

Tell me that I don't need to be a Mother -

Tell me that I'll be a good Mother.

Tell me I won't have to do it all.

Tell me the weight of our union won't break on my shoulders.

Tell me you won't leave me, that you won't fall away from me –

Tell me the promise I'm about to make will not be a school yard pinky promise –

Broken by the time class begins.

Tell me the words "I do",

So I can echo them back.

Lie next to me.

Lie next to me and tell me I'm strong.

Lie next to me and tell me I'm the strongest man you've ever met.

Sit next to me.

Sit next to me and tell me I'm confident.

No –

Sit next to me and tell me *you're* confident in *me*.

Tell me you think I can do anything.

Tell me you respect me.

Tell me you think I'm as powerful as Superman,

As smart as Einstein.

Tell me that you believe in me.

Stand next to me.

Stand next to me and tell me you need me.

Tell me you want me more than any other man you've ever wanted.

Tell me that you won't leave me and that you will be by my side when things get tough.

Stand next to me and take my hand

And tell me I don't always have to be strong.

Stand next to me

And tell me that when I'm not the strongest man you'll be the strongest woman.

Stand next to me.

Stand next to me and tell me that when I'm unsure

You will always have the answer.

Tell me I can be confident in you.

Tell me I won't have to do everything.

Tell me I won't have to be as powerful as Superman or as smart as Einstein.

Stand next to me, and tell me you love me.

Tell me that there is and never will be another man.

Tell me that the weight of this union will not break on my shoulders.

Stand next to me.

Stand next to me and tell me

You do.

<u>Please Excuse me, I'm not Feeling Beautiful Today</u>

Please excuse me, but I'm not feeling beautiful today.

You see, my hair is much too short for my liking –

So I will hide the length as well as I can.

Please excuse me, but I'm not feeling beautiful today.

My face is rather dry, and the facial lotion only
aggravates it so I don't think I'll put any on –

Maybe I'll just stay home today…the world will just
have to wait.

Please excuse me, but today, my beauty does not seem
as radiant as it was the day before.

So today I will take a picture. I will edit and edit and
edit until I see yesterday's beauty on today's face.

Today I will post a picture, and I will write a false
self-deprecating statement – maybe something like:

omg just woke up sooo exhausted #collegelife
#feelingtired #goingnatural

Today I will make sure that today's photo exceeds
yesterday's perfection.

Did I say perfection?

I meant beauty.

Please, excuse me, but I'm not feeling perfect today.

I mean, beautiful.

T
R
I
U
M
P
H
A
N
T

<u>I Have The Champion's Blood in my veins</u>

There is success in every breath I breathe;

I have The Champion's Blood coursing through my veins.

Watch out for my punches- I'm not here to play games.

Watch my feet-

Fast and swift they move-

Blink and I'm already miles ahead.

I have The Heart of The Lion-

Beating in my chest-

These are not scars from failed struggles-

They are from

Victorious Battles.

I have The Sword Of The King-

And the fist of a fighter-

Watch out world, here I come.

Every tear is a hard won diamond-

See this Light emanating from my chest?

It is Strong and Fierce-

Like a cheetah on the prowl-

And He will destroy all that comes against.

<u>No longer victims</u>

You are no longer a victim.

To your circumstances, to your past –

Your past is not who you are

Your past does not define you.

And I know –

That you have heard all this before that you have seen the motivational posters that you have seen the Facebook posts and I know that you're thinking "I have heard this a *million* times."

But I will tell you a million times more.

I will tell you over and over and over again. I will shout it, yell it, whisper it, write it, proclaim it -

I will not stop until you *get* it.

I will not stop reminding you of your brilliant future.

I will not stop until you *get* it until the light bulb is turned on until sun floods your mind until the relief blows through your heart

that

you

are

not

a

victim.

And I know -

That things have happened.

And I know -

That life didn't always go the way you planned.

But

you

are

Not

a

victim.

Whatever happened to you, whatever you are going through, I am here to tell you that you are *not* subjected to them you are *not* chained down to them you are *not* dependent on them

You

owe

them

nothing.

Your life

Your future

Your joy

Your peace

is yours to keep.

Not to feed to your past.

You are not a victim.

You

Are

a

Victor.

You are the Warrior looking across the field of fallen
foes you are standing Victorious over all of your hurt
and pain and you are the Victor –

On a crystal throne -

Reminding the world that you are a Winner -

And you never settle for any less.

You

Are

a

Victor.

And I will tell you, over and over and over again.

Because I love you too much -

To see you walk through life defeated.

<u>Not Built For Losing</u>

I'm not built for losing.

I wasn't made to lose the battles I face.

I was built to win.

I was built to destroy – my doubts – my fears -

I was created to conquer – my trials – my troubles –

I don't always choose my fights –

But I always choose to win.

I don't care how strong you say my opponent is –

I say I wasn't built to lose.

And I say I will win.

And win.

And win.

And win

And I will keep on winning because that is what –

I was built to do.

You were built to win.

Every fight,

Every battle,

Every problem,

You were designed to conquer.

You were designed to obliterate every obstacle in your path.

Because you –

Are a conqueror

You

Are a winner

You are –

Much more than you know.

So shake off the dust –

And pick up your sword.

Now go out and

Win.

<u>I'm a Fighter (And in heels, no less)</u>

I'm a boxer.

I do not have the gloves or the shoes-

But I have the strength.

I have the fire.

I do not lose.

I may get hit-

But I do not lose.

I am not alone in this fight.

My Father is in my corner, cheering me on.

I am more than a conqueror.

I will not be defeated.

I am strong.

I am powerful.

My Father stands behind me-

Not only to catch me when I fall-

But to embrace me when I win.

<u>Battle Cry</u>

I will give pep talks to myself.

I will remind myself that I'm a strong warrior –

A fierce Victor –

A Triumphant Victor.

Made for more.

Dear one you were made for more.

More than whatever your situation may be

You were created –

Yes, created -

I said created -

For so much more.

Let this be your pep talk.

Let this be your Battle Cry.

<u>In Case No One Has Told You</u>

You matter.

You are important.

You were made for a purpose.

You were made for great things.

You have a great future.

You are loved.

You are treasured.

You are precious.

You are special.

You are unique.

You are powerful.

You have dreams.

You have hope.

You are strong.

You are wonderful.

And in case no one has told you,

I love you.

<u>Perseverance</u>

I have made up my mind –

To not move –

When trials come.

I have made up my mind –

To be as strong as an oak.

I have made up my mind

To be as fierce

As a hurricane.

I

Will be the eye in the storm

I

Will be the calm

I

Will be in peace during the chaos.

Because I have made up my mind –

To reject

That which is not life.

I have made up mind –

To reject

All that is not

Life.

I only have room

For Life in this heart.

I only have room

For

Joy

In this heart.

This heart –

Is not my own.

This heart –

Belongs To

Another.

And I will not let

This heart be tainted –

With the debris of a storm.

With fear.

No.

My heart

Will be the calm –

Felt by the mother after giving birth.

I will be

The mother holding her newborn child

Healthy and strong.

And I will smile and say:

"It is well"

Because

I have prevailed.

I choose brave.

I choose fierce –

Cause when things get tough I don't *get* tougher –

I *am* tougher.

When the going gets tough I rise up and yell that I'm tougher than tough that I thrive in tough that tough has nothing on my strength.

When things get hard I laugh –

Because I know the Power I have.

I know the diamond I am inside.

I know that diamonds can withstand the pressure and the heat –

And they don't break.

So I don't break.

When things get difficult I smile,

Because I can bend –

Like bamboo.

Because I know the light in my Spirit I know the burning zeal in my heart I know that these coals never expire.

Kindling upon kindling keeps my heart going.

Flame upon flame burns the troubles around me.

I choose bold –

I choose life –

I choose fire.

I choose the heat in the knuckles of a boxer –

I choose the impact of a fist crashing through a wall -

I choose the sweat dripping down the face of a Champion -

I *choose* the joy of gold.

Golden gloves and golden heart –

I'm a champion –

A diamond in the sun.

<u>Sprinting</u>

I'm not afraid of the future.

I'm running towards it.

Full speed ahead.

You dare challenge my heart?

You dare question my strength?

Watch me fly –

No

Watch me soar.

Watch me run.

Faster than the doubts, faster than the fears, faster than the worries.

Watch me seize the future.

Watch me grab it, hold it, and treasure it.

Watch me wrestle it into the future that I want.

Watch me fight. And fight. And fight and then –

Watch me win.

Watch me climb onto the podium and accept my gold medal.

Watch my future dazzle.

Watch it shine brighter than a million suns at noon.

Watch my future smile –

Watch His teeth sparkle.

Watch My future take my hand and hold me tight and pull me close and say –

"I have prepared all this for you."

Watch me walk on water.

Watch me glide on air.

I'm sprinting,

And with each step I move faster.

The future is mine.

<u>I Don't Want This To Be Interpreted</u>

I don't want this to be interpreted.

I don't want teachers to assign this to their students and
ask them to find the theme, the tone, the voice –

I don't want this to be interpreted.

I don't want people to spend hours figuring out the
message.

I don't want this to be interpreted.

I don't want –

This poem to be read aloud –

And for people in the audience to clap

And turn their heads to whisper:

"I don't get it. It must be good."

No.

I don't want this to be interpreted.

I don't want people to groan when reading this.

I want them to know exactly what I'm saying.

I want them to understand

How wonderful their life was created to be.

So this is what I'm saying:

"I want you to know that your future is bright.

I want you to know that no matter what you think,
your life is important because you are very important.

I want you to know that you have beautiful and
extraordinary things to do in your life.

I want you to know that you were made on purpose for
a purpose.

I want you to know that you were made for more than
your current situation.

I want you to know that there is always Hope.

I want you to know that there will always and forever
be Hope."

I don't want this to be interpreted.

<u>To The Dreamers</u>

It is time –

To look up.

It is time to –

Revive –

What has been sleeping for far too long.

Inside of you –

Is a dream.

I know it's there.

I know it was placed inside you.

And whether you put it aside or forgot about it or told
yourself that it didn't matter -

That's a lie.

Because your dreams, your hopes, they *do* matter they
are the jewel inside your heart, it is the hope in the
breaking dawn, it is the Light that was placed inside
you, deep inside you, and I know you can see it dear
one, feel the Light dear one, see the Light dear one -

I know you can.

I know you have a dream.

And even if someone pushed it aside for foolishness,

Even if someone dismissed it as *nothing* –

I'm here to tell you -

That

they

were

Wrong.

That dream is *something* it is something *good* because
you are something *good* and *you* are not nothing you are
everything and you have that dream because it is *good*.

It is time

To restore.

It is time to

Dig deep in your heart

And rekindle that fire.

I know that you have a dream inside.

So now

It is time to find it -

Revive it -

And bring it to the Light again.

Your dreams

Are far too precious

To be locked away.

And you

Are far too precious

To still be hiding.

Dear one,

It is time to breathe Life again.

<u>the bibliography</u>

Empowerment (https://www.merriam-webster.com/dictonary/empowerment, accessed 1/2/19)

<u>about the author</u>

Rachel Dowdell is a passionate writer, poet, and novelist.

As an insightful and introspective woman, Dowdell often uses her writing to reflect on hard-hitting, controversial, and deeply personal topics— topics that cut to the core of what it means to be human. In her debut as a published poet, she offers her unique perspective as a young, bi-racial woman, boldly calling attention to the juxtapositions and tensions she feels as she struggles to find her identity and determine her purpose in a complex and confusing world.

Throughout her journey, she challenges her readers to address their own fears and shortcomings, as she faces her own, all the while inspiring hope for the future and empowering her readers to take control of their destiny.

When she's not writing, Dowdell can often be found sipping a good cup of coffee, perusing a bookstore, or baking up a storm in her home kitchen. While she loves the fresh country air of the Vermont mountains, Dowdell now resides in the bustling Boston Area and is enjoying city life as she finishes her undergraduate degree.